GOLDFISH

Carmady is a private detective. He works alone, and there's enough crime in the city of Los Angeles to keep him busy most of the time. He makes mistakes – who doesn't? – but all the bullets have missed him so far.

When Kathy Horne comes into his office with a story about the long-lost Leander pearls, Carmady doesn't think much of it at first. But Kathy's a friend. There's a $25,000 reward for anyone who finds the pearls, and Kathy needs some money for when her husband gets out of prison. So Carmady goes on listening.

There's a guy called Peeler Mardo, Kathy says. He was in prison one time and he met the guy who stole the Leander pearls from the mail-car. And this guy, Wally Sype, had too much to drink one night and told Peeler where the pearls were hidden.

So Carmady goes to talk to Peeler Mardo. But he's too late, as Peeler Mardo isn't going to do any more talking – ever. He's already talked too much, Carmady realizes, and it's a long journey, a lot of bullets, a lot of dead bodies, before anyone gets near those pearls.

And where do the goldfish come into the story?

OXFORD BOOKWORMS LIBRARY
Crime & Mystery

Goldfish

Stage 3 (1000 headwords)

Series Editor: Jennifer Bassett
Founder Editor: Tricia Hedge
Activities Editors: Jennifer Bassett and Christine Lindop

To Jane
for so many things

RAYMOND CHANDLER

Goldfish

Retold by
Christine Lindop

Illustrated by
Terry Hand

OXFORD UNIVERSITY PRESS

OXFORD
UNIVERSITY PRESS

Great Clarendon Street, Oxford OX2 6DP

Oxford University Press is a department of the University of Oxford.
It furthers the University's objective of excellence in research, scholarship,
and education by publishing worldwide in

Oxford   New York

Auckland   Cape Town   Dar es Salaam   Hong Kong   Karachi
Kuala Lumpur   Madrid   Melbourne   Mexico City   Nairobi
New Delhi   Shanghai   Taipei   Toronto

With offices in

Argentina   Austria   Brazil   Chile   Czech Republic   France   Greece
Guatemala   Hungary   Italy   Japan   Poland   Portugal   Singapore
South Korea   Switzerland   Thailand   Turkey   Ukraine   Vietnam

OXFORD and OXFORD ENGLISH are registered trade marks of
Oxford University Press in the UK and in certain other countries

ISBN 978 0 19 479117 5

Printed in Hong Kong

Word count (main text): 10,100 words

For more information on the Oxford Bookworms Library,
visit www.oup.com/elt/bookworms

CONTENTS

The Leander pearls

I was sitting in my office, busy doing nothing. No phone calls, no messages. Nobody in Los Angeles seemed to need a private detective today.

A warm wind blew in at the window, bringing with it the smell of the oil-burners from the hotel opposite.

I was just thinking about going to lunch when Kathy Horne came in.

Kathy was a tall blonde with sad eyes who had once been a policewoman. She lost her job when she married a cheap little crook called Johnny Horne, hoping to make him into an honest man. Now Johnny was back in prison again, and Kathy worked at the Mansion House Hotel across the road, selling cigars, and waiting to try again with Johnny.

She sat down and lit a cigarette.

'Did you ever hear of the Leander pearls?' she asked. 'God, that old blue suit of yours is so shiny. You must have money in the bank, the clothes you wear.'

'No,' I said, 'to both your ideas. I never heard of the Leander pearls, and I don't have any money in the bank.'

'Then maybe you'd like to make yourself a cut of twenty-five grand.'

I put my cigarette out. How was Kathy Horne going to put her hands on twenty-five thousand dollars?

'Did you ever hear of the Leander pearls?' Kathy asked.

'It was nineteen years ago,' Kathy went on. 'A guy up north named Sol Leander bought the pearls for his wife – just two of them. They cost two hundred grand.'

'How can you wear something as big as a football?' I asked.

'I see you don't know a lot about pearls,' Kathy said. 'It's not just how big they are. Well, they're worth more now, and the insurance company is still offering a reward of twenty-five grand for them.'

'Ah, I get it,' I said. 'Somebody stole them.'

'Now you're using your head. It was a mail-car robbery. A guy hid on the train, got into the mail car and shot the clerk. Then he took all the valuable mail and got away. But when they caught him later in Canada, they didn't get any of the stuff. They sent him to Leavenworth prison for life, but they never proved he got the pearls.'

'If it's going to be a long story, let's have a drink.'

'I never drink before sunset,' Kathy said. She watched me get my little flat bottle out, then went on, 'His name was Sype – Wally Sype. He did it alone. And he never said anything about the stuff that he took. After fifteen years they offered him a pardon, but he had to tell them where the stuff was. So he gave them everything – except the pearls.'

'Where was it?' I asked. 'In his hat?'

'Listen, this isn't just a funny story, Carmady,' Kathy said. 'I've got a lead to those pearls.'

I shut my mouth with my hand and looked serious.

'Sype said he never had the pearls, and I guess they believed him, because he got the pardon. But the pearls were on the train, and they were never seen again.

'Just once in Leavenworth prison Sype had too much to drink and started talking. The guy that he told was a little man called Peeler Mardo. Sype said he'd hidden the pearls somewhere in Idaho.'

I sat forward a little.

'Getting interested, eh?' Kathy said. 'Well, listen to this. Peeler Mardo rents a room in my house and he drinks too much and he talks in his sleep.'

I sat back and sighed. 'Oh Kathy,' I said. 'For a moment I was planning how to spend that reward money.'

Kathy looked coldly at me. Then her face changed. 'All right,' she said, a little hopelessly. 'Maybe it's a crazy idea. It was a long time ago, and a lot of people have looked for those pearls. But he's a nice little guy, and I believe him. He knows where Sype is.'

'Did he say all this in his sleep?'

'Of course not. But you know me. An old policewoman's got ears. I guessed he was an ex-con, and sometimes I stopped outside his door and listened to him talking to himself. When I'd heard enough, I made him tell me the rest. He wants help to get that insurance money.'

I sat forward again. 'So where's Sype?'

Kathy smiled. 'He refused to tell me that, or the name that Sype's using now. But it's somewhere up north, near Olympia, Washington. Peeler saw him there, and he says Sype didn't see *him*.'

I lit another cigarette and had another little drink.

'OK,' I said. 'Will he talk to me? I guess he wants help with talking to the insurance company. After, of course, he goes to see Sype, and Sype just puts the pearls straight into his hand and walks away. Is that it?'

Kathy sighed. 'Yes, he'll talk to you,' she said. 'But he's really frightened about something. Will you go and see him?'

'Sure – if that's what you want.'

Kathy took her keys out of her bag and wrote her address

on a piece of paper. She stood up slowly.

'I live in one side of the house, and Peeler has a room in the other side. There's a door between the two sides, with the key on my side. If he won't come to the door, you can get in that way.'

'OK,' I said. I blew smoke at the ceiling and looked at her.

I blew smoke at the ceiling and looked at her.

Kathy walked towards the door, stopped, and came back. She looked down at the floor.

'This is Peeler's business, really,' she said. 'And yours now. But if I could have a grand or two waiting when Johnny came out, then maybe—'

'Maybe you really could keep him honest,' I said. 'It's a dream, Kathy. It's all a dream. But if it isn't, you get a third, with Peeler and me.'

Kathy opened her mouth in surprise, then stared hard at the window, to stop herself from crying. She went towards the door, turned and came back again.

'That isn't all,' she said. 'It's the old guy – Sype. He did fifteen years in prison. That's a long time. Doesn't it make you feel bad?'

I shook my head. 'He stole the pearls, didn't he? He killed a man. What does he do now?'

'His wife has money,' Kathy said. 'He spends all his time with his goldfish.'

'Goldfish?' I said. 'To hell with him.'

Kathy went out of the door.

A body and a reward

Kathy's house was on a corner, high up on a hill. It had been two houses once, so it had two front doors. I rang the bell on Mardo's side, but nobody came. Then I went to the other door. Nobody answered.

While I was waiting, a grey Dodge car went quickly round the corner and a smart girl in blue looked up at me for a second. I didn't see the other person in the car. I didn't look very hard. I didn't know it was important.

I opened the door with Kathy's key, and walked in to a living-room with just enough furniture in it. I walked through the house until I found the door to the other side. I unlocked it and went through.

At the back of the house I found a room with a closed door. No answer. I went in. The little man on the bed was probably Peeler Mardo. I noticed his feet first, because they were tied to the end of the bed by a rope round the ankles.

Somebody had burned the bottoms of his feet until there was no skin left. There was still a smell of burning in the room, and on a table by the bed there was a hot electric iron. I turned it off.

I went to Kathy's kitchen and found some whiskey. I drank some of it and looked out of the window. Then I went back to Peeler Mardo's room.

Peeler was wearing a shirt and trousers. On the bed next to him was the stuff from his pockets – some keys and some money.

He was a little man, no taller than one meter sixty, with thin brown hair and large ears. His eyes weren't blue or brown or green. They were just eyes, very open, and very dead. His arms were tied by ropes to the bedhead.

I looked for bullet holes, but there was nothing.

I looked for bullet holes, but there was nothing. It was just the burns. I suppose his heart stopped when they put the iron on his feet. He was still warm.

I cleaned everything that I had touched, looked out of Kathy's front window for a while, then left the house.

○ ○ ○

It was three-thirty when I walked into the cigar shop in the Mansion House Hotel and asked for a packet of cigarettes.

Kathy gave me the smile that she kept for customers. 'You didn't take long,' she said, passing me the packet.

'It's serious,' I told her. 'Are you ready for this?'

She looked past my head, her eyes cool and empty.

'I'm ready,' she said.

'You get half the money,' I said. 'Peeler's dead. He was bumped off – in his bed.'

Kathy's eyes moved a little, and a white line showed around her mouth. That was all.

'Listen,' I said. 'Don't say anything until I've finished. Somebody burned his feet with an electric iron. I think he probably died quickly and didn't say very much. When I went there, I didn't believe this story, but now I'm not so sure. If he told them anything, we're finished, and so is Sype, if I don't find him first. If he didn't, there's still time.'

Kathy looked towards the hotel door. Her face was white.

'What do I do?' she said very quietly.

I dropped her keys into a box of cigars. In a moment her long fingers had taken them and hidden them.

'When you get home, you find him. You don't know

anything. Don't talk about the pearls, don't talk about me. When they find out he's an ex-con, they'll think it was something from his past.'

I opened the packet of cigarettes and lit one. I watched Kathy, but she didn't move.

'Can you do it?' I asked. 'If you can't, tell me now.'

'Of course I can do it,' she said. 'Do I look like the kind of person who could do that with an iron?'

'You married a crook,' I said.

'He isn't a crook!' she answered, her face turning pink. 'He's just a bit stupid sometimes. Nobody thinks the worse of me because of him.'

'All right. It's not our murder, after all. And if we say anything now, we'll never get any of that reward – if there ever is one.'

'You're right there,' said Kathy. 'Oh the poor little guy,' she said, her voice breaking.

I touched her arm gently, smiled and left the Mansion House Hotel.

○ ○ ○

The Reliance Insurance Company had offices in the Graas Building, three small rooms that looked like nothing at all. The manager was named Lutin – a middle-aged bald man with quiet eyes and small thin fingers.

'Carmady, eh? I've heard of you.' He touched my business card with his little finger. 'What's your problem?'

I took out a cigarette and spoke quietly. 'Remember the Leander pearls?'

His smile was slow, a little bored. 'Remember them? They cost this company one hundred and fifty thousand dollars. Sure I remember them.'

I said, 'I've got an idea. Maybe it's a bit crazy – in fact it probably is. But I'd like to try it. Is your twenty-five grand reward still good?'

He laughed. 'Twenty grand, Carmady. But it's not worth your time.'

'It's my time. Twenty it is, then. How much help can I get?'

'What kind of help?'

'Can I have a letter that I can take to your other offices? Or show to the police if I need to?'

'Which offices? Which police?'

I smiled at him, and he smiled back. Neither of our smiles was honest.

'No letter,' he said. 'We can't put anything on paper. The New York office wouldn't like it. But we'll give you all the help that you want. And the twenty grand, if you find the pearls. But you won't, of course. Not after twenty years.'

I lit my cigarette and blew smoke at the ceiling.

'It's still my own time,' I said.

He looked at me for a moment. 'Suppose I send somebody to follow you? What then?'

'I'll know if that happens. I've done this job for too long. I'll tell the police what I know, and go home.'

'The police? Why?'

I put my hands on the desk. 'Because,' I said slowly, 'the guy that had the lead got bumped off today.'

11

I smiled at him, and he smiled back.
Neither of our smiles was honest.

'Oh – oh.'

'I didn't bump him off,' I said.

We were both silent for a while. Then Lutin said, 'You don't want a letter. And now you've told me that, you know I won't give you one.'

I stood up, smiled, and started walking towards the door. He ran around the desk and put his hand on my arm.

'Listen, Carmady, I know you're crazy, but if you do get anything, bring it to us. It'll look good for the business.'

'It'll look good for me too,' I said. 'And my business.'

'Twenty-five grand.'

'I thought it was twenty.'

'Twenty-five. And you're still crazy. Sype never had the pearls – I'm sure of it.'

'OK,' I said. 'You've had plenty of time to think about it.'

We shook hands and smiled, both pretending to be honest men. I didn't believe him, and he didn't believe me.

○ ○ ○

It was a quarter to five when I got back to the office. I had a couple of short drinks, and then the phone rang.

A woman's voice said, 'Carmady?' It was a small, cold voice. I didn't know it.

'Yeah.'

'You need to see Rush Madder. Know him?'

'No,' I lied. 'Why should I see him?'

There was a laugh like the sound of breaking ice. 'Because of a guy who had sore feet,' the voice said.

The call ended. I put the phone down, lit a match and stared at the wall until I burned my fingers.

Rush Madder was a crook in the Quorn Building. He was a lawyer who did dirty work, anything that smelled a little and paid a little more. But burning people's feet didn't sound like Rush Madder's kind of business to me.

13

A drink with Rush Madder

On Spring Street people were finishing work, but I had a job to do. The Quorn Building was a narrow, dirty yellow building. On the wall by the door, between the names of people who could fix your teeth painlessly and people who didn't want to say what they did, I found the name of Rush Madder. He was in Room 619.

Everything in the Quorn Building was old and tired and smelled of yesterday's cigarettes. The door of Room 619 was locked. I knocked.

The door opened noisily and I was looking at a big man with a round face, oily skin, and a thin black moustache.

He put out two yellow fingers. 'Well, well, the old dog-catcher himself. Carmady is the name, I believe?'

I followed him into a room with no carpet, a desk and three chairs. There was a clothes closet and a washbowl in the corner by the door.

'Sit down,' Madder said. 'Pleased to see you. Nice of you to come. Business?'

I sat down, put a cigarette between my teeth and looked at him. I didn't say a word. He started to get worried. He looked up at me quickly, then down again.

'Any ideas?' he asked softly.

'About what?'

He didn't look at me. 'About how we could do a deal together.'

'Who phoned me?' I asked.

'Did somebody phone you?'

I reached for his telephone, picked it up, and very slowly began to put in the number of the Los Angeles Police Station. I knew Madder would know the number as well as I did. He reached over and pulled the phone back.

Madder reached over and pulled the phone back.

'You're too fast,' he said. 'What are you calling the cops for?'

'They want to talk to you,' I said slowly. 'Because you know a woman who knows a man who had sore feet.'

'Does it have to be that way?' He looked hot, and pulled his shirt open at the neck.

'No – but only if you stop playing with me and start talking.'

'OK, calm down,' said Madder, putting a cigarette in his mouth with a shaking hand.

'So talk,' I said. 'If you've got a job, it's probably too dirty for me to touch. But I can listen.'

He was calmer now. 'The thing is this,' he said. 'Carol saw you go to the house and leave it again, but no cops came.'

'Carol?'

'Carol Donovan. Friend of mine. She phoned you.'

'Go on,' I said.

He didn't say anything, just sat there and looked at me.

I smiled. 'This is your problem,' I said. 'You don't know why I went to the house or why I didn't call the cops afterwards. That's easy. I thought it was a secret.'

'We're just kidding each other,' Madder said.

'OK, let's talk about pearls,' I said. 'Does that make it easier?'

Madder was trying hard not to get excited. He said in a low voice, 'Carol met the little guy one night. He was drinking too much, but he had this story about pearls, about an old guy in Canada who stole some pearls a long time ago and still had them. But he wouldn't say who the old guy was or where he was. I don't know why.'

'He wanted to get his feet burned,' I said.

Madder's lips shook. 'I didn't do that,' he said.

'You or Carol, what does it matter? The little guy died. It's still murder. And you didn't find out what you needed to know. That's why *I'm* here. You think I have information that you didn't get. But listen. Why do you think I came? Same reason as you. We're both looking for information. Right?'

He grinned, very slowly. He opened the desk and took out a brown bottle and two glasses. He whispered:

'Here's the deal, Carmady. We'll cut it two ways – you and me. Not Carol. I don't like the way she does things. I've seen hard women, but this one is as hard as a rock. She doesn't look it, but she is.'

'Have I seen her?'

'She says you did.'

'Oh, the girl in the Dodge.'

He put plenty of whiskey in the glasses and stood up. 'Water? I like it in mine.'

'Why cut me in?' I said. 'I don't know any more than you.'

'I can get fifty grand for the Leander pearls, but I need you to do the job. How about the water?'

'No water,' I said.

He went to the washbowl, put water in his glass, and came back. He sat down and grinned.

We drank.

○ ○ ○

So far I had only made four mistakes. The first was agreeing to help Kathy. The second was staying on the job after I found Peeler Mardo dead. The third was with Rush Madder – I knew what he was talking about, and I let him see it. The fourth, the whiskey, was the worst.

It tasted strange even on the way down. Suddenly I knew that Madder had taken one glass of whiskey to the washbowl and come back with a different one. His drink was whiskey and water, but mine was whiskey and something nasty.

I sat still for a moment and tried to think. Madder grinned as he watched me.

I put my hand in my pocket and pulled out a small sap. Then I stood up and hit Madder on the top of the head with it. When he tried to get up, I hit him again. As he fell, he knocked his glass over. I stood still, listening, and feeling sick and sleepy.

I put a chair against the door to keep it shut. I was just walking back towards Madder when the door of the closet opened and a very pretty girl stepped out and pointed a gun at me.

She wore a smart blue suit with a little blue hat. She had shiny black hair and her eyes were dark grey, and cold. Her face was young and bright and pretty and as hard as stone.

'All right, Carmady. Lie down and go to sleep. You're finished.'

I tried to walk towards her, my sap in my hand. The floor seemed to move under my feet.

'Don't be stupid, Carmady,' she said. 'A few hours' sleep

*A very pretty girl stepped out of the closet
and pointed a gun at me.*

for you, a few hours' start for us. Don't make me shoot. I will if I have to.'

'I believe you,' I said. My voice sounded slow and thick.

'That's right. Now sit down,' she said.

The floor came up and hit me. I put my hands out, but I couldn't feel very much. Far away I heard a cold laugh, and strange lights and shadows moved in front of my eyes. I didn't want to lie down. I lay down.

The girl's voice came from very far away.

'Cut it two ways, eh? He doesn't like the way that I do things, eh? We'll see about that.'

I was going – I was almost gone, when I felt something. Was it a shot? I hoped she had shot Madder, but she hadn't. She had hit me – with my own sap.

○ ○ ○

The next thing I knew, it was night. Through the window I could see a yellow light going on and off, on and off. I got up off the floor and walked over to the washbowl with heavy feet. I threw some water on my face, then turned on the light.

On the floor by the desk there were papers, cigarette ends, an empty whiskey bottle. I didn't stop to look at any of it. I left the office, stopped in a bar for a drink, got my car and drove home.

I changed my clothes, packed a bag, had some whiskey, and answered the phone. It was about nine-thirty.

Kathy's voice said, 'So you haven't gone yet.'

'Alone?' I asked, my voice still thick.

'I am now, but the house was full of cops for hours. They were very nice. Thought it was some problem from his past.'

'Listen, Kathy – I haven't gone yet, but where was I going?'

'Oh – you know. Your girl told me.'

'A little dark girl? Name of Carol Donovan?'

'Well, yes. She had your card. Wasn't she—?'

'I don't have a girl,' I said. 'And – don't tell me – when you were talking to Carol, you said a name – the name of a town up north. Did you?'

'Ye-es,' Kathy said.

I caught the night plane north. It was a nice trip, but my head hurt and I was very, very thirsty.

Looking for goldfish

I left the Snoqualmie Hotel in Olympia and walked down to the water. This quiet, lonely place was right at the end of Puget Sound, and a long way from the sea. Under the grey-blue sky a few old men sat around on boxes, smoking their pipes and selling firewood.

I sat down on a box next to an old man who wore an old raincoat. I filled my pipe, lit it, and looked around me.

'I like this place,' I said to the old man. 'It's quiet and restful – I like that.'

He looked at me.

'Someone like you – you must know everybody in this town and round about,' I said.

'What's it worth?' he said.

I took a silver dollar out of my pocket and the old man looked at it.

'I don't know everybody,' he said.

I put the dollar on my knee. 'Know anybody that keeps a lot of goldfish?' I asked.

A second old man, wearing shoes but no socks, came over and stared at the dollar. The first man turned his head and shouted, 'Know anybody that keeps goldfish?'

'Finish? Finish it yourself!' screamed the second man, and walked away.

22

'His ears aren't so good,' said the first man. He walked off to a small office, went in and slammed the door. A minute later he opened it again.

'Mexican chickens. That's all.'

I put my dollar back in my pocket and went back up the hill. I didn't have enough time to learn their language.

I walked along Capitol Way, past shops and hotels. Then I turned left and crossed a bridge, and suddenly I was in a part of town where the buildings were old and dirty – a cinema with no films, an empty restaurant. A sign above my head said 'Smoke Shop'. I looked through the window and saw a tall thin man with a long nose, playing pool all by himself. This was Peeler's kind of place, I thought.

I walked in and sat down. A bald man with hard eyes got up from a chair behind the bar.

'I'll have a whiskey,' I said. 'Know anybody that keeps goldfish?'

'Yes,' he said. 'No.'

He passed me a glass. The whiskey was very new and tasted like something you cleaned your boots with.

'This stuff is new in town then,' I said.

The barman put his hands heavily on the bar and stared at me. 'What did you say?' he asked.

'I'm new in town,' I said. 'I'm looking for some goldfish to put in my front window. Goldfish.'

The barman said slowly, 'Do I look like a guy who knows a guy who has goldfish?' His face was a little white.

The man with the long nose stopped playing pool and

'I'm looking for some goldfish to put in my front window,' I said.

walked over to the bar. 'Get me a drink,' he said. The barman took his big fingers off the bar (he left no holes in it – I looked) and put a drink on the bar. Then he walked away.

The long-nosed man picked up his drink. 'How's Peeler?'

I took an empty glass from the bar, stared down into it, and shook my head slowly and sadly.

'Still drinking too much, huh?'

'Yes,' I said. 'I didn't catch your name.'

'Call me Sunset. I'm always moving west. Think he'll keep quiet?'

'Sure he will,' I said.

'What's your name?'

'Dodge Willis, El Paso,' I said.

'Got a room somewhere?'

'Hotel.'

He put his glass down empty. 'Let's go.'

○ ○ ○

We went up to my room and sat down and looked at each other over a glass of whiskey. Sunset studied me carefully, while I drank my whiskey and waited. At last he said,

'Why didn't Peeler come himself?'

'For the same reason that he didn't stay when he was here.'

'What does that mean?'

'Think it out for yourself.'

He nodded, and seemed to find some meaning in my answer. Then he said, 'How much?'

'Twenty-five grand.'

'Huh!'

I lit a cigarette and watched the smoke go slowly out of the open window.

'Listen,' Sunset said. 'I don't know you. You could be anybody at all.'

'So why did you come and talk to me?' I asked.

'You had the word, didn't you?'

I took a chance. I grinned at him. 'Yeah, Goldfish was the word, and the Smoke Shop was the place.'

His face didn't change, so I knew I was right. It was one of those pieces of luck that you dream about, but never get.

'Well, what happens next?' Sunset asked.

I laughed. 'OK, Sunset, we could go on like this for weeks. Where is the old guy?'

Sunset didn't say anything, but he put his glass down

'You're kidding the wrong guy,' Sunset said.

very slowly. I knew I had made a mistake. Peeler knew where the old guy was, so I should know too.

Nothing in Sunset's voice showed that I had made a mistake. He said crossly: 'You mean why don't I just tell you everything I know, and you say thank you? Forget it.'

'Well, how do you like this?' I said. 'Peeler's dead.'

A corner of his mouth moved. His eyes were even emptier than before.

'How did that happen?'

'There was some competition that you two didn't know about.' I smiled at him.

I didn't see where the gun came from. Then the end of the gun was looking at me like a round dark eye.

'You're kidding the wrong guy,' Sunset said.

'I'm not kidding anybody. Peeler told a girl about it, but he didn't tell her where to find the old guy. So she and her top man went to see Peeler. They used a hot iron on his feet. It killed him.'

Sunset looked bored. 'Keep talking – I've got a lot of room in my ears yet.'

'So have I,' I said, suddenly pretending to be angry. 'What the hell have you said that means anything – except that you know Peeler? Got any more to tell me?'

He played with his gun. 'Old man Sype's at Westport,' he said. 'Does that mean anything to you?'

'Yes. Has he got the pearls?'

'How should I know?' He put down the gun. 'Where's this competition that you talked about?'

'I hope I got away from them, but I'm not sure,' I said.

'And who's giving you a cut?' Sunset asked.

'Peeler rented a room from a friend of mine – she's honest, I know she is. He told her, and she told me – afterwards.'

'So how many cuts are there?'

'Three – you, me and her. If we can stop the competition.'

'What are they like, this competition?'

'He's called Rush Madder, a crook lawyer down south, aged fifty, fat, thin moustache, dark hair, one meter seventy-five, a bit soft. The girl, Carol Donovan, black hair, grey eyes, pretty, aged about twenty-five, one meter sixty, made of stone. She's the real hard man of the pair.'

Sunset put his gun away. 'We can soften her,' he said. 'I've got a car at my place. Let's go over to Westport and look around. Maybe you can talk to him about goldfish. They say he's crazy about them. I'll stay out of the way. I've been in prison, and he'll know it.'

'That's OK with me,' I said. 'I just love goldfish.'

Sunset reached for the whiskey bottle. He put a little whiskey in his glass and then drank it. Then he stood up.

'Don't make any mistake,' he said. 'This isn't going to be easy. Maybe we'll have to take Mr Sype for a ride to a lonely place. Maybe we'll have to take the stuff and run.'

'That's OK,' I said. 'The insurance company are behind me.'

I put my hat on, put the whiskey in my bag, and closed the window.

We were walking towards the door when somebody

knocked on it. I waved at Sunset to stay behind the door. I stared at the door, then I opened it.

There were two guns at the door, one small, one big. The girl came in first.

'OK, big guy,' she said. 'See if you can touch the ceiling.'

There were two guns at the door, one small, one big.

A meeting at Sunset's

I backed slowly into the room, and the two visitors came with me, one on each side. My bag was in the way, and I fell over it and hit the floor.

Sunset said, 'Hands in the air.'

Two heads suddenly turned to look at Sunset, and then I had my gun out, down at my side. There was a silence. I didn't hear any guns fall. The door was still wide open and Sunset was flat against the wall behind it.

The girl said between her teeth: 'Keep your gun on him, Rush – and shut the door. Nobody can shoot here.' Then, in a whisper that I could just hear, she said, 'Slam it!'

Rush Madder walked backwards across the room, still pointing his gun at me. His back was to Sunset. He was not happy about that, but Sunset was almost smiling.

Sunset stared at the girl and she stared at him. Their guns stared at each other.

Rush Madder reached the door, took hold of the edge of it, and pushed it hard. I knew what was going to happen. When the door slammed, the girl's gun was going to go off – and nobody would hear it.

I reached for Carol's ankle and pulled it hard. The door slammed. Her gun went off and hit the ceiling.

She turned on me, kicking wildly.

Sunset said, 'If this is it, this is it. Let's go!' He lifted his gun.

Something in his voice calmed her. She stepped back, and let her gun fall to her side. Madder turned the key in the door.

Nothing happened. Nobody came to the door. I put my gun away, got up and looked out of the window. Nobody outside was interested in us.

Carol said angrily to me, 'Is this guy working with you?'

I didn't answer. Her face slowly went red and her eyes

I reached for Carol's ankle and pulled it hard.

burned with anger. Madder put out a hand and said, 'Now listen, Carol. This isn't the way—'

'Shut your mouth!'

'Yeah, sure,' Madder said.

Sunset looked at the girl lazily. He looked very calm.

He said slowly, 'We've heard about you two. What are you offering?'

The girl said, 'There's enough in it for four.' Madder nodded quickly.

Sunset looked at me. I nodded. 'Four it is,' he sighed, 'but no more. We'll go to my place for a drink. I don't like it here.'

Carol took a bag from under her arm and put her little gun in it. She smiled. She was pretty when she smiled.

'OK,' she said. 'I'll join you. Where is your place?'

'Out on Water Street. We'll go in a taxi.'

'Let's go then.'

We went out of the room and down in the lift, and walked out of the hotel like four friends.

○ ○ ○

The taxi took us along Capitol Way, past the town buildings. We turned onto a road that went towards the water, and soon we came to a house between tall trees. There was an untidy garden in front of it, and a very old car at the side.

We got out and I paid the taxi. Sunset said, 'My place is upstairs. There's nobody at home down below. Let's go up and have a drink.'

He threw open the door and pointed up the steps. 'Ladies first. Go on, beautiful. Nobody locks a door in this town.'

The girl gave him a cool look and went in. I went next, then Madder, and Sunset last.

We went up into a big room with a bed, a table, some chairs, and a radio. Sunset went into a small kitchen and came back with a bottle and some glasses.

We each took a glass and sat down.

Sunset drank his drink, put his glass down on the floor, and brought his hand up holding his gun.

There was a sudden cold silence and I saw Madder's mouth turn white. Carol moved her lips in a kind of smile. Then she sat forward, holding her glass on top of her bag with her left hand.

Sunset said slowly and carefully, 'Burned my friend's feet, huh? And you're stupid too. You burn a guy's feet to make him talk, then you walk right into his friend's house. Well, maybe it's Christmas, and you're the present.'

Madder's fat hands were shaking a little. 'All r-right,' he said. 'What – what are you going to do to us?' The girl smiled a little, but she didn't say anything.

Sunset grinned. 'Do?' he said softly. 'I think I'll tie you up with rope, really hard. Then me and my friend'll go looking for some pretty stones – pearls to you – and when we come back—' he stopped, and pulled his finger across his neck. 'Like the idea?' he said to me.

'Yeah, but don't make a song about it,' I said. 'Where's the rope?'

'In the cupboard,' said Sunset, and pointed with one ear at the corner.

I started walking to the cupboard. Suddenly Madder made a little thin noise and his eyes turned up in his head and he fell forward off his chair in a faint.

That made Sunset jump, and his right hand moved round until his gun was pointing down at Madder's back.

The girl put her hand under her bag. The gun that she had hidden there made a short, sudden noise.

Sunset's gun fell out of his hand. His head fell back, and his face tried to look at the ceiling. His long legs went out in front of him, and he sat like that, his head back and his eyes looking up. Dead as a burnt match.

'Get up,' I said.

I kicked the girl's chair out from under her, and she fell off it onto her side. I stood on her hand and then kicked her gun across the room. I kicked her bag after it – with her other gun inside it. She screamed at me.

'Get up,' I said.

She got up slowly and backed away from me to the wall, with a crazy light in her eyes, and showing her teeth like a wild animal.

I went over to a door. There was a bathroom behind it. I waved my hand at Carol.

'In.'

She walked across the floor and in front of me, very close.

'Listen a minute—'

I pushed her through the door, slammed it and turned the key. The bathroom had a window and she could jump out, but I didn't care.

I went across to Sunset and felt his pockets. There were some keys on a ring, and one of them was a car key.

I looked at Madder, noticed that his fingers were as white as snow, then went downstairs and out of the house. I got into the old car and put the key in the lock. It fitted.

It took a while before I could get the car started and drive it down to the road. Nothing moved in the house. The tall trees around it waved in the wind, and a cold heartless sunlight shone through their branches as they moved.

I drove as fast as I could back to Capitol Way, past the Snoqualmie Hotel, and over the bridge towards the sea and Westport.

At Sype's house

I drove Sunset's tired old car as fast as I could for an hour and a half. Then I was in Westport, a quiet little place with houses here and there on a green hill, and sailing boats on the blue sea. This was as far west as you could go in the United States. It was a good place for an ex-con to hide with pearls that were not his – if he had no enemies.

I stopped in front of a small house with a sign that said, 'Lunches and dinners.' In the garden a little man was arguing with some chickens. The chickens were winning. I got out, walked to the garden and pointed to the sign. 'Is lunch ready?'

He looked up at the sign. 'Lunch? That means ham and eggs,' he said.

'That's fine with me,' I said.

We went into the house. I sat down at a table and the little man went off to the kitchen. He came back with a knife and fork, and put them on the table.

'Too early for a drink, isn't it?' he whispered.

I told him how wrong he was, and he went away and came back with glasses and a bottle. I could hear food cooking and a deep voice singing in the kitchen.

We drank.

'Stranger, aren't you?' the little man asked.

I said I was.

'From Seattle, maybe? That's a nice suit you're wearing.'

'Seattle,' I agreed.

'We don't get many strangers here,' he said. 'It's not on the way to anywhere. What brings you here?'

'I'm looking for goldfish,' I said. 'I'm a goldfish buyer. Have another drink – I'm paying.'

He grinned. 'What did you say your name was?'

'Carmady. And I'm not kidding about the goldfish.'

'There's no money in goldfish, is there?'

I held out my arm. 'You see this nice suit? Goldfish paid for that. There's new kinds of fish all the time, and people always want to buy something new. Now I heard there was an old guy here with hundreds of fish. Maybe he's got some new ones, and he'd like to sell some of them.'

A large woman with a moustache opened the kitchen door and shouted, 'Ham and eggs.'

The little man brought my food to the table. I ate. He watched me. After a while he suddenly banged his hand on his knee. 'Old Wallace,' he said grinning. 'Sure, you've come to see old Wallace. We don't know him very well. He's not very neighborly.'

He pointed past the dirty curtains to a yellow and white house on top of a hill.

'That's where he lives. He's got lots of them.'

That ended my interest in the little man. Now I just wanted to leave. I ate my food quickly, paid for it, shook the man's hand, and went out to the car.

I was in no hurry. When Rush Madder woke up, he would

37

let the girl out, but they knew nothing about Westport. Sunset had not talked about it when they were with us. I had lots of time. I went down to the sea and looked at the fish for sale. There were some bars and a pool-room and a few people with nothing much to do. I didn't see any cops.

I drove up the hill to the yellow and white house. There were no other houses nearby. In the garden a woman in a brown and white dress was cutting flowers.

I got out of the car and took my hat off.

'Mister Wallace live here?'

She was a good-looking woman, quiet and strong. She nodded.

'Would you like to see him?' Her voice was quiet and strong too – not the voice of a train-robber's wife.

I gave her my name and told her I was interested in goldfish.

She went into the house. I looked around me. The air was cold and clear and smelled of the sea, but the northern sunshine felt cool on the skin and had no heat in it.

The woman came out again and held the door open.

'He's at the top of the stairs,' she said, 'if you'd like to go up.'

I went into the house of the man who had stolen the Leander pearls.

○ ○ ○

There were fish tanks all around the big room, some with lights over them and some with lights in them. The water in them held a ghostly greenish light, and through the greenish light moved fish of every color that you can think of.

There were long thin golden fish, and Japanese Veilfish with fantastic tails. There were tiny fish one centimeter long, and fish that you could see through. There were big black Chinese Moors, with great round eyes and long fins, swimming through the water like fat men going to lunch.

Most of the light came from a window in the roof. Under

There were fish tanks all around the big room,
containing fish of every color that you can think of.

the window a tall thin man stood at a wooden table, holding a red fish in one hand and a knife in the other. He looked at me with eyes that told me nothing.

I went over to him and looked down at the fish he was holding.

'Fungus?' I asked.

He nodded slowly. 'White fungus.' He put the fish on the table. The edge of the fin on its back was white.

'White fungus,' he said, 'isn't so bad. I'll cut it off and this fish will be fine. What can I do for you, Mister?'

I played with a cigarette and smiled at him.

'Like people,' I said. 'The fish, I mean. They get things wrong with them.'

He held the fish against the wood and cut away the white edges of its fins. The fish was still.

'Some things you can fix, and some you can't,' he said. He put some purple stuff on the cut edges of the fins, and put the fish into a small tank. It swam around peacefully.

The thin man dried his hands, sat down and stared at me. He had been good-looking once.

'You interested in fish?' he said. He had the quiet voice of an ex-con.

I shook my head. 'Not really. It's you I came to see, Mister Sype.'

He went on staring at me. Then he said in a soft, tired voice, 'Wallace is the name, Mister.'

I blew a smoke ring.

'For my job it has to be Sype.'

He sat forward and brought his hands together – strong, hard hands that had done a lot of work in their time. His voice was still soft.

'Haven't seen a dick in a year. What's your story?'

'Guess,' I said.

'Listen, dick. I've got a nice home here. I get no trouble from anybody, and that's how it should be, because I got my pardon from the White House. I've got my fish, and that's enough for me. My wife's got enough money for both of us. All I want is to be left alone.'

I didn't say anything. I smiled a little and watched him.

'Nobody can touch me,' he said. 'I got my pardon. I just want to be left alone.'

I shook my head and smiled. 'That's the one thing that you can never have – until you tell.'

'Listen,' he said softly. 'Maybe this is all new to you. Well, I've had almost twenty years of this, and a lot of other people – clever people – have too. *They* know I've got nothing that doesn't belong to me. Never did. Some other person got it.'

'The mail clerk,' I said. 'Sure.'

'Listen,' he said, still softly. 'I did my time in prison. I know people aren't going to stop wondering. I know that from time to time somebody is going to come along with some questions. That's OK. Now how do I get you to go home again?'

I shook my head and stared at the fish in their big silent tanks, thinking about ghosts – ghosts from a long time ago. A train moving through the darkness, the sound of shooting,

'All I want is to be left alone,' said Sype.

a dead clerk on the floor, a man who had kept a secret for nineteen years – almost kept it.

○　○　○

'You made one mistake,' I said slowly. 'Remember a guy called Peeler Mardo?'

I could see him thinking, trying to remember.

'A guy that you knew in Leavenworth prison,' I said. 'You told him you had the pearls.'

I could see he didn't believe me. 'I was kidding him,' he said slowly.

'Maybe – but he didn't think so. He was up here with a

friend, a guy called Sunset. Peeler recognized you, and he started thinking about making himself some money. But he drank too much and he talked in his sleep. A girl heard about it, then another girl and a guy that works with her. Peeler got his feet burned and he's dead.'

Sype stared at me. I went on:

'We don't know how much he said, but the girl and her guy are in Olympia. So is Sunset, but he's dead. They killed him. Maybe they know where you are, maybe they don't. But they will some time. Somebody will always find you. When the cops stop looking and the insurance company isn't interested any more, there'll always be some crooks who've heard a story about a guy with some pearls. And they'll find out what they want to know. They'll take your wife, and they'll take you out to the forest for a talk . . . Now I've got an honest deal for you.'

'Who are you?' Sype asked suddenly. 'I thought you were a dick, but I'm not so sure now.'

'Insurance,' I said. 'Here's the deal. Twenty-five grand reward. Five grand to the girl who gave me the lead. Ten grand for me. I've done all the work, and I've looked into all the guns. Ten grand to you. You can't get it without me. What do you say?'

'Fine,' he said, 'but I haven't got any pearls, dick.'

I had no more to say. I dropped my cigarette on the floor and stood on it. I turned to go.

He stood up and held his hand out. 'Wait a minute,' he said, 'and I'll prove it to you.'

He went out of the room. I stared at the fish. Somewhere, not very close, I heard a car engine. I heard the sound of something shutting in a nearby room.

Sype came back into the fish room. He had a big gun in his hand.

'I've got pearls in this – six of them,' said Sype.

He pointed it at me and said, 'I've got pearls in this, six of them. You're not a dick. Now get out of here – and tell your friends I'm ready to shoot their teeth out any day of the week and twice on Sunday.'

I didn't move. There was something crazy about the man's dead eyes.

'Stop acting,' I said. 'I can prove I'm a dick. You're an ex-con and you shouldn't have that gun. Put it down and talk sensibly to me.'

The car that I had heard was stopping outside the house. I heard feet on the steps, sudden voices.

Sype went backwards across the room until he was between the table and a big tank. He grinned at me.

'So your friends have found you,' he said. 'Take your gun out and drop it on the floor – while you've still got time.'

I didn't move. I looked into his eyes, and kept very still. He was ready to shoot me for moving a finger.

There were feet on the stairs. Some of them belonged to people who didn't want to come up the stairs.

Three people came into the room.

Black fish, white pearls

Mrs Sype came in first. I could see that she didn't want to be there. There was a strange look in her eyes, her elbows were close to her sides, and her hands felt in front of her for something that was not there. There was a gun in her back, one of Carol Donovan's small guns, held in Carol's small hand. Carol had a job to do, and she didn't care about Mrs Sype.

Madder came last. He was full of whiskey, which made him brave, and his stupid little eyes shone in his red face. He pointed his gun at me and grinned nastily.

Carol Donovan pushed Mrs Sype to one side. The older woman fell down on her knees in the corner, her eyes empty of feeling.

Sype stared at the Donovan girl. She was a girl and young and pretty, and he didn't know what to do about it. He had never known girls like that. He could shoot men to pieces, but a pretty girl . . .

The small dark white-faced girl stared at him coldly, and said in her hard little voice:

'All right, Dad. Put the gun down. No surprises now.'

Sype didn't take his eyes off her. Slowly he put his big heavy gun on the floor.

'Kick it away from you, Dad.'

Sype kicked it. The gun went across the wooden floor and stopped near the middle of the room.

'That's right, Dad. You hold him, Rush, while I get the dick's gun off him.'

The two guns turned and the hard grey eyes were looking at me now. Madder went a little closer to Sype and pointed his gun at Sype's stomach.

The girl smiled, not a nice smile. 'Clever boy, eh? You really go looking for trouble, don't you? But you made a mistake. Your thin friend had a little map in his shoe, and you didn't find it.'

'I didn't need one,' I said, and grinned at her.

I tried to make it the kind of grin that would keep her looking at me, because Mrs Sype was moving slowly across the floor on her knees, getting closer and closer to Sype's gun all the time.

'You're finished now, you and your big smile. Put your hands up while I get your gun. Up, Mister.'

She was a girl, about one meter sixty tall, and about fifty-five kilos. Just a girl. I was one meter eighty, and nearly twice as heavy. I put my hands up and hit her on the head.

That was crazy, but I was sick of the Donovan–Madder guns, the Donovan–Madder talk.

She stepped back and her gun went off. A bullet burned my side. She started to fall, very slowly. It seemed unreal.

Mrs Sype got Sype's gun and shot her in the back.

Madder turned quickly and at once Sype jumped towards him. Madder jumped back and shouted and pointed his gun at Sype again. Sype stopped, and the big crazy grin came back onto his face.

The bullet from Sype's gun had knocked the girl forward, and her head hit my body. I saw her face for a moment as she fell back again to the floor – a strange face that I had never seen before.

Then she was on the floor at my feet, small, deadly, and dead, with redness coming out from under her, and the quiet woman behind her on her knees, with the smoking gun held in her hand.

Madder shot Sype twice. Sype fell forward, still grinning, and hit the end of the table. The purple stuff he had used on the sick fish went all over him. Madder shot him again as he was falling.

I pulled out my gun and shot Madder in a place that would be painful but wouldn't kill him – the back of the knee. He dropped to the floor. I put handcuffs on him before he even started to make a noise.

I kicked some guns away and went over to Mrs Sype and took the big gun out of her hands.

It was very still in the room for a little while. A little grey smoke from the guns went slowly up to the window in the roof. I heard the sound of the sea on the wind outside. Then I heard another sound nearby.

It was Sype trying to say something. His wife went to him, still on her knees. There was blood on his lips. He smiled up at her and said very quietly:

'The Moors, Hattie – the Moors.'

Then Carol was on the floor at my feet, small, deadly, and dead.

Then the smile disappeared from his face and his head fell to one side on the wooden floor.

Mrs Sype touched him, then stood up very slowly and looked at me calmly, with dry eyes.

She said in a low clear voice, 'Will you help me carry him to the bed? I don't like him here with these people.'

'Sure,' I said. 'What was that he said?'

'I don't know. Something about the fish, I think. It doesn't matter.'

I lifted Sype's shoulders and she took his feet and we carried him into the bedroom and put him on the bed. She crossed his hands over his body and shut his eyes. She went over and closed the curtains.

'That's all, thank you,' she said, not looking at me. 'The telephone is downstairs.'

She sat down in a chair beside the bed and put her head down on the bedcover near Sype's arm.

I went out of the room and shut the door.

◦ ◦ ◦

Madder's leg was bleeding slowly, but he was not in danger. He stared at me, crazy with fear, while I stopped the bleeding. He would walk again. Maybe not as well as before, but well enough to climb the steps one day to a man who waited with a rope, ready to put it around his neck.

I went downstairs and stood looking at the two cars, then down the hill towards the sea. I didn't think anybody had noticed the shots. There was probably a lot of shooting in the woods around there.

I went back into the house and looked at the telephone, but didn't touch it yet. Something was worrying me. I lit a cigarette and stared out of the window and a ghost voice said in my ears, 'The Moors, Hattie. The Moors.'

I went back upstairs into the fish room. Madder was making a lot of noise now, but what did I care about him?

The girl was dead. None of the tanks was hit. The fish swam peacefully in their green water, slow and peaceful and easy. Like me, they didn't care about Madder.

The tank with the black Chinese Moors in it was over in the corner. There were four of them, big fish, about ten centimeters long, as black as the night. Two of them were at the top of the tank and two were moving slowly around at the bottom. They had thick deep bodies, a lot of tail, high fins and big eyes.

I watched them for a moment. The two fish on the bottom looked thicker and moved more slowly than the ones at the top. I wondered why.

There was a small net next to the tank. I used it to catch one of the big Moors and lift it out. I looked at it carefully. There on its stomach was something that looked like a suture. I felt the place. There was a hard lump under it.

I caught the other fish from the bottom. Same suture, same lump. I got one of the black Moors from the top of the tank. No suture, no lump, and it was harder to catch.

I put it back in the tank. My business was with the other two fish. I like goldfish, but business is business and crime is crime. I took my coat off and picked up the knife.

The job took about five minutes, and it was not pretty. Then I held them in my hand – about two centimeters across, heavy, round, milky white and shining with that beautiful light that belongs only to them. The Leander pearls.

I washed them, put them in a piece of paper, and put my coat back on. I looked at Madder, his eyes full of pain and fear. I didn't care about Madder. He was a killer.

I went out of the fish room. The bedroom door was still shut. I went downstairs and picked up the phone.

I caught the other fish from the bottom. Same suture, same lump.

'This is the Wallace place at Westport,' I said. 'There's been an accident. We need a doctor and we'll need the police. What can you do?'

The girl said: 'I'll try and get you a doctor, Mr Wallace, but it may take a little time. There's a town marshal at Westport. He's the nearest thing to the police round here. Will that be all right?'

'I suppose so,' I said. I thanked her and put the phone down.

○ ○ ○

I lit another cigarette and sat down on one of the chairs outside the front door. In a little while Mrs Sype came out of the house. She stood for a moment looking out across the hills, then she sat down in the other chair. Her dry eyes looked at me calmly.

'You're a detective, I suppose,' she said.

'Yes. I'm working for the company that insured the Leander pearls.'

She looked away. 'I thought he would have peace here,' she said. 'That people would leave him alone.'

'He tried to keep the pearls. That was wrong.'

She turned her head quickly. She looked afraid.

I took the piece of paper out of my pocket and opened it. There they were, two hundred grand worth of murder.

'Peace?' I said. 'Nobody wanted to take that away from him. But it wasn't enough for him.'

She looked slowly, hungrily at the pearls. Her voice sounded dry and hard.

'Poor Wally,' she said. 'So you did find them. You're kind of clever, you know. He killed an awful lot of fish before he learned how to do that.' She looked up into my face.

She said, 'I always hated the idea. But Wally had to do it.'

She smiled at me. I didn't smile back.

She said, 'You see, he once had the pearls, the real ones, and he felt they were his. But when he came out of prison, he couldn't find the place where he had hidden them.'

I felt an icy finger moving up and down my back. Something – was it my voice? – said, 'Huh?'

53

She reached a finger out and touched one of the pearls. I was still holding them out.

'So he got these,' she said. 'In Seattle. They're clever, don't you think? They look very fine – just like the real thing. Of course I never saw any really valuable pearls.'

'What did he get them for?' I asked. My voice was almost a whisper.

'Don't you see? They were his crime. He wanted to remember what he had done, and what he had done it for, and all those long years that he spent paying for it. Hiding the pearls in the fish was a way of remembering, and a way of punishing himself. And do you know—' Her eyes were shining, and she spoke very slowly:

'Sometimes I think that in the very end, he really believed they were the real pearls that he was hiding. Does all this mean anything to you?'

I looked down at the pearls. My hand closed over them slowly.

I said, 'I'm nothing special, Mrs Sype. I guess that idea is a bit too hard for me. I think he was just trying to kid himself.'

She smiled again. She was good-looking when she smiled. Then she said lightly:

'Of course, you would think that. But me – oh well, it doesn't matter much now. May I have them, to remember him with?'

'Have them?'

'The – the phony pearls. Surely you don't—'

'May I have them, to remember him with?' said Mrs Sype.

I stood up. An old Ford car without a top was coming noisily up the hill. The man driving it had a big star on his shirt.

Mrs Sype was standing next to me, with her hand out. The look on her face said how much she wanted the pearls.

I grinned at her in sudden anger.

'Yeah, you were very good in there for a while,' I said. 'I almost believed you. I had a cold feeling all down my back, lady! But you helped. "Phony" was the wrong kind of word for you to use. And you were too good and too fast with that gun. But most of all it was Sype's last words. "The Moors, Hattie – the Moors". You don't use your last words for something that isn't real. And he wasn't stupid enough to kid himself all the way.'

For a moment her face didn't change at all. Then it did. Something nasty showed in her eyes. Then she went into the house and slammed the door.

I put twenty-five thousand dollars safely into my pocket. Twelve thousand five hundred for me and twelve thousand five hundred for Kathy Horne. I could see her face when I brought her the cheque, and when she put it in the bank, to wait for Johnny to come out of prison.

The Ford had stopped behind the other cars. The man driving climbed out. He was a big guy wearing a shirt, no jacket.

I went down the steps to meet him.

GLOSSARY

believe to think that something is true or right

blonde a woman with yellow or golden hair

bump off *(informal)* to murder somebody

clerk a person who works in a bank, office, or store

closet *(American)* a cupboard with a door that you can walk into

competition people who want something that you want too

cop *(informal)* a police officer

crook *(informal)* a dishonest person or a criminal

cut *(n)* a share in something, usually money

deal *(n)* an agreement about how to do something

dick *(informal, American)* a detective

ex-con *(informal)* someone who has been to prison

faint *(n)* a kind of 'sleep' caused by shock, illness, etc.

fungus something unhealthy that grows on the skin

go off *(of a gun)* to be fired

goldfish a small orange or red fish, kept as a pet

grand *(n) (informal)* one thousand dollars

grin to smile widely

guy *(informal)* a man

handcuffs metal rings put around the wrists of a prisoner

hell (to hell with) *(informal)* words that show you are angry or
    do not care about something

insurance money paid to a company, which then pays you if
    your car is stolen, your house burns downs, etc. *(v)* **insure**

kick *(v)* to hit something or someone with the foot

kid *(v) (informal)* to say something that is not true, often as a joke

lawyer someone whose job is helping people with the law

lead *(n)* information that helps you to find out the truth about
    something, especially a crime

lump a solid piece of something under the skin
marshal *(American)* an officer who works for the law courts
moustache the hair above a man's mouth, below his nose
nasty bad, not nice
net pieces of string tied together, used for catching fish
nod to move your head up and down to say yes
oil a thick liquid that is burned to give heat
pardon *(n)* when a prisoner gets a pardon, they are allowed to leave prison early
pearl a very valuable jewel (a small hard shiny white ball found inside oysters)
phony *(informal)* false, not real
point *(v)* to show with your hand or finger where something is
pool a game played by hitting sixteen coloured balls on a table
private working for yourself, not for the government
prove to use the facts to show that something is true
rent to pay somebody money to use a house, shop, etc.
reward money that you get for finding something that is lost
sap *(informal, American)* a small heavy stick used as a weapon
sigh *(v)* to breathe out slowly when you are sad, tired, etc.
sign a piece of wood or metal with writing or pictures that give information
slam *(v)* to shut with a loud noise
smart well dressed or fashionable
sore painful
stuff *(informal)* things that people do, say, think, etc.
sunset the time when the sun goes down and night begins
sure *(informal, American)* yes, of course
suture a piece of thread used to sew up a wound
yeah *(informal)* yes

Goldfish

ACTIVITIES

Before Reading

1 Read the story introduction on the first page of the book, and the back cover. What do you know now about the story? Choose T (True) or F (False) for each sentence.

1 Carmady works for the Los Angeles police. T / F
2 The Leander pearls were stolen a month ago. T / F
3 The person who finds the pearls will get $25,000. T / F
4 Peeler Mardo found out about the pearls when he was in prison. T / F
5 Wally Sype stole the pearls from the mail-car. T / F
6 Peeler dies after he talks to Carmady. T / F

2 What do you think will happen in the story? Cross out what you think probably will *not* happen.

1 Carmady *will / will not* find the pearls.
2 *Two / Four / Six / Eight* people will die.
3 The pearls will be found *on a boat / in a house / under the ground / in a garden.*
4 Somebody will *hit / shoot / kill* Carmady.
5 Six people will know about the pearls, but *none / one / two / three* of them will get the reward.

3 Why do you think the title of this story is *Goldfish*?

ACTIVITIES

While Reading

Read Chapters 1 and 2. Match these people with the sentences. (You can use the names more than once.)

Peeler Mardo / Carmady / Lutin / Sol Leander / Rush Madder / Kathy / Wally Sype

1 _____ once worked for the police.

2 _____ bought two pearls for $200,000.

3 _____ now lives near Olympia.

4 _____ was in prison with the man who stole the pearls.

5 _____ left prison after fifteen years.

6 _____ found _____ dead in _____'s house.

7 _____ thought _____ was crazy and would never find the pearls.

8 _____ was a lawyer but also a crook.

Before you read Chapter 3, can you guess what will happen in Rush Madder's office? Choose as many ideas as you like.

1 Carmady will agree to work with Madder.

2 Madder will give Carmady some useful information.

3 Carmady will hit Madder.

4 Carmady will meet the woman who phoned him.

5 Somebody will hit Carmady.

6 Carmady will shoot somebody.

Read Chapters 3 and 4. Are these sentences true (T) or false (F)? Rewrite the false sentences with the correct information.

1 Rush Madder offered Carmady a three-way deal.
2 Carol did not hear what Madder and Carmady were saying.
3 Carol told Kathy that she worked with Carmady, and Kathy believed her.
4 Carmady went into the Smoke Shop because he wanted to buy some goldfish.
5 Carmady did not give his real name to Sunset.
6 Sunset knew where Sype was living, but he did not tell Carmady.
7 Sunset thought it would be easy to get the pearls from Sype.
8 Sunset was crazy about goldfish.
9 The big gun and the small gun at the door were carried by Rush Madder and Carol Donovan.

Before you read Chapter 5, what do you think will happen after Carmady, Sunset, Carol and Madder meet? Use this table to make as many sentences as you like.

		dead.
Carmady		tied up.
Madder		on foot.
Sunset	will leave the hotel	in a police car.
Carol		alone.
		in an ambulance.
		with a gun in his/her back.

Read Chapters 5 and 6, then match these halves of sentences.

1 When Carol whispered 'Slam it!', . . .
2 When Madder fell off his chair in a faint, . . .
3 When Carmady left Sunset's house, . . .
4 From the little man at Westport, Carmady learned . . .
5 Carmady thought he had lots of time in Westport . . .
6 Sype told Carmady that he didn't have the pearls, . . .
7 Carmady offered Sype a deal on the insurance money, . . .
8 Sype was pointing his gun at Carmady . . .
9 that Sype was using the name 'Wallace'.
10 and that all he wanted was to be left alone.
11 Sunset jumped, and Carol shot Sunset and killed him.
12 when three people came up the stairs and into the room.
13 Carmady knew that she was planning to shoot somebody.
14 because Carol and Madder did not know where Sype lived.
15 but Sype still said that he hadn't got any pearls.
16 Carol was locked in the bathroom and Madder was still
    lying on the floor in a faint.

How will the story end? Before you read Chapter 7, try to guess the answers to these questions. Choose from these names for your answers.

Sype / Carmady / Mrs Sype / Carol / Rush Madder / Kathy

At the end of the story . . .
1 who will be alive?
2 who will have the pearls?
3 who will get the reward?

After Reading

1 **Perhaps this is what some of the characters in the story are thinking. Which five characters are they, and what is about to happen in the story?**

   1 'There's something funny about this guy. First he doesn't know where the old guy lives, and now he says Peeler's dead. Time to get serious, I think . . .'

   2 'So you don't know any more than we do, eh? Right, time for that special glass of whiskey. And then we'll leave you sleeping here while we're on our way north . . .'

   3 'Does he believe me? Oh, I do hope so. I mean, who would put real ones inside a fish? Come on – just take them out of that paper and put them in my hand . . .'

   4 'He's back quickly. And he looks so serious – he's got bad news written all over his face. Perhaps he's found out what Peeler was so frightened of . . .'

   5 'Why can't they leave me alone? That's all I want. I need to stop this guy coming back with his friends. Right, here it is. I'll show him this, and tell him I'm ready to use it . . .'

   6 'What's going on out there? Nobody's speaking. And that sounded like somebody falling over. But who? It's no use – I'll have to come out and see what's happening . . .'

2 Here is part of Carmady's report about what happened at
Sype's place. Complete it using the linking words below. (Use
each word once.)

*although / and / and / and / and then / as / before / but /
in order to / so / then / then / which / while*

_____ I grinned at Carol, Mrs Sype was moving across the
floor _____ get her husband's gun, _____ was near the middle
of the room. _____ I hit Carol on the head, _____ Mrs Sype
shot her in the back. Madder shot Sype twice, _____ he shot
him again _____ he was falling to the floor. I wanted to hurt
Madder, _____ I didn't want to kill him, _____ I shot him in
the back of the knee. _____ he could get up again, I put
handcuffs on him, _____ took the gun away from Mrs Sype.
_____ I heard Sype's voice. _____ he was dying, he smiled at
his wife _____ told her to remember the Moors.

3 Here is Carmady, phoning Kathy with the news. Complete the
passage with suitable words (one word for each gap).

'Great news, Kathy, I found the _____! And you'll never
_____ where I found them – inside two _____. No, I'm not
_____ – that _____ money is ours! Just think, twelve and a
half _____ each. With that much, maybe your _____ will
come true and you really can keep Johnny _____. No, don't
worry about the _____. Carol's _____, and the _____ have
taken Madder away in _____. Me? Oh, maybe I'll buy myself
a new _____ – what do you think, Kathy?'

4 There are 19 words (3 letters or longer) from the story in this word search. Find the words and draw lines through them. They go from left to right, and from top to bottom.

C	O	M	P	E	T	I	T	I	O	N	H
O	M	A	E	A	Y	F	I	N	B	A	A
P	E	I	A	I	R	T	S	S	C	S	N
H	R	L	R	I	E	S	G	U	Y	T	D
F	T	L	L	A	W	Y	E	R	M	Y	C
A	C	U	T	K	A	A	S	A	A	N	U
I	D	M	Y	I	R	O	K	N	U	S	F
N	R	P	E	D	D	T	I	C	H	I	F
T	E	P	R	O	V	E	C	E	P	G	S
R	E	S	C	R	O	O	K	E	N	H	T

5 Look at the word search again and write down all the letters that don't have a line through them. Begin with the first line and go across each line to the end. You should have 35 letters, which will make 7 words.

   1 What are the words, and who said them?
   2 Where was he, and who was he talking to?
   3 What did he mean?

6 When Madder comes out of his faint at Sunset's place, he finds himself alone with a dead body, while Carol is locked in the bathroom. Complete Carol's side of their conversation.

   MADDER: Oh, I feel bad. What . . .? Who's that shouting?
   CAROL: _____

MADDER: Carol? Where are you? What's the matter?

CAROL: _____

MADDER: Yeah, OK, OK, I'm coming. But what happened? Who locked you in? Are you OK?

CAROL: _____

MADDER: And what about this guy here? He's dead! Who – who shot him, Carol?

CAROL: _____

MADDER: You're a hard woman, Carol. So then it was just you and the dick. Why didn't you shoot him too?

CAROL: _____

MADDER: And then he went off to find the pearls. So what do we do now? How are we going to find him?

CAROL: _____

MADDER: Yeah, good idea. I'll search the room, you search the – er – the body.

CAROL: _____

MADDER: OK, OK, no need to shout. I'll help you . . .

7 **Here are some different titles for the story. Some are better than others. Can you say why?**

- Carmady Goes Fishing
- Kathy's Dream
- A Tank Full of Secrets
- The Hidden Pearls
- The Mail-Car Robbery
- The Mail-Car Pearls
- A Guy with Sore Feet
- Kathy and Carmady

Now explain which title you like best, or think of a title of your own for the story.

ABOUT THE AUTHOR

Raymond Chandler was born in Chicago, in 1888, but moved to England with his mother when he was twelve. He went to school in London, and later worked as a newspaper reporter and book reviewer. In 1912 he returned to America, and went to live in California. After the First World War, during which he was in the Canadian army, he did a number of different jobs, and then worked for an oil company. He married in 1924.

Like his detective Philip Marlowe, Chandler had a problem with drinking, and he lost his job with the oil company because of it. He began writing detective stories, and his first story, *Blackmailers don't Shoot*, was published in *Black Mask* magazine in 1933. Over the next six years, Chandler continued to learn the craft of writing stories, always with a male detective. The character known as 'Carmady' in *Goldfish* would one day become Chandler's most famous creation, Philip Marlowe. In 1939 his first novel, *The Big Sleep*, appeared, and it was an immediate success. In his later novels, including *Farewell, My Lovely* (1940), *The High Window* (1942), *The Lady in the Lake* (1943), and *The Long Goodbye* (1953), Chandler frequently re-used parts of his earlier stories. He enjoyed great success from his writing, but after his wife's death in 1954 his health became poor, and he died in California in 1959.

Raymond Chandler is one of the great writers of crime fiction. He described the detective-hero like this: 'He must be a complete man and a common man and yet an unusual man . . . He must be the best man in his world and a good enough man for any world.'

OXFORD BOOKWORMS LIBRARY

Classics • Crime & Mystery • Factfiles • Fantasy & Horror
Human Interest • Playscripts • Thriller & Adventure
True Stories • World Stories

The OXFORD BOOKWORMS LIBRARY provides enjoyable reading in English, with a wide range of classic and modern fiction, non-fiction, and plays. It includes original and adapted texts in seven carefully graded language stages, which take learners from beginner to advanced level. An overview is given on the next pages.

All Stage 1 titles are available as audio recordings, as well as over eighty other titles from Starter to Stage 6. All Starters and many titles at Stages 1 to 4 are specially recommended for younger learners. Every Bookworm is illustrated, and Starters and Factfiles have full-colour illustrations.

The OXFORD BOOKWORMS LIBRARY also offers extensive support. Each book contains an introduction to the story, notes about the author, a glossary, and activities. Additional resources include tests and worksheets, and answers for these and for the activities in the books. There is advice on running a class library, using audio recordings, and the many ways of using Oxford Bookworms in reading programmes. Resource materials are available on the website <www.oup.com/elt/bookworms>.

The *Oxford Bookworms Collection* is a series for advanced learners. It consists of volumes of short stories by well-known authors, both classic and modern. Texts are not abridged or adapted in any way, but carefully selected to be accessible to the advanced student.

You can find details and a full list of titles in the *Oxford Bookworms Library Catalogue* and *Oxford English Language Teaching Catalogues*, and on the website <www.oup.com/elt/bookworms>.

THE OXFORD BOOKWORMS LIBRARY
GRADING AND SAMPLE EXTRACTS

STARTER • 250 HEADWORDS

present simple – present continuous – imperative –
can/cannot, must – *going to* (future) – simple gerunds ...

Her phone is ringing – but where is it?

Sally gets out of bed and looks in her bag. No phone. She looks under the bed. No phone. Then she looks behind the door. There is her phone. Sally picks up her phone and answers it. *Sally's Phone*

STAGE 1 • 400 HEADWORDS

... past simple – coordination with *and*, *but*, *or* –
subordination with *before*, *after*, *when*, *because*, *so* ...

I knew him in Persia. He was a famous builder and I worked with him there. For a time I was his friend, but not for long. When he came to Paris, I came after him – I wanted to watch him. He was a very clever, very dangerous man. *The Phantom of the Opera*

STAGE 2 • 700 HEADWORDS

... present perfect – *will* (future) – *(don't) have to, must not, could* –
comparison of adjectives – simple *if* clauses – past continuous –
tag questions – *ask/tell* + infinitive ...

While I was writing these words in my diary, I decided what to do. I must try to escape. I shall try to get down the wall outside. The window is high above the ground, but I have to try. I shall take some of the gold with me – if I escape, perhaps it will be helpful later. *Dracula*

... should, may – present perfect continuous – *used to* – past perfect –
causative – relative clauses – indirect statements ...

Of course, it was most important that no one should see
Colin, Mary, or Dickon entering the secret garden. So Colin
gave orders to the gardeners that they must all keep away
from that part of the garden in future. *The Secret Garden*

STAGE 4 • 1400 HEADWORDS

... past perfect continuous – passive (simple forms) –
would conditional clauses – indirect questions –
relatives with *where/when* – gerunds after prepositions/phrases ...

I was glad. Now Hyde could not show his face to the world
again. If he did, every honest man in London would be proud
to report him to the police. *Dr Jekyll and Mr Hyde*

STAGE 5 • 1800 HEADWORDS

... future continuous – future perfect –
passive (modals, continuous forms) –
would have conditional clauses – modals + perfect infinitive ...

If he had spoken Estella's name, I would have hit him. I was so
angry with him, and so depressed about my future, that I could
not eat the breakfast. Instead I went straight to the old house.
Great Expectations

STAGE 6 • 2500 HEADWORDS

... passive (infinitives, gerunds) – advanced modal meanings –
clauses of concession, condition

When I stepped up to the piano, I was confident. It was as if I
knew that the prodigy side of me really did exist. And when I
started to play, I was so caught up in how lovely I looked that
I didn't worry how I would sound. *The Joy Luck Club*

The Last Sherlock Holmes Story

MICHAEL DIBDIN

Retold by Rosalie Kerr

For fifty years after Dr Watson's death, a packet of papers, written by the doctor himself, lay hidden in a locked box. The papers contained an extraordinary report of the case of Jack the Ripper and the horrible murders in the East End of London in 1888. The detective, of course, was the great Sherlock Holmes – but why was the report kept hidden for so long?

This is the story that Sir Arthur Conan Doyle never wrote. It is a strange and frightening tale . . .

Chemical Secret

TIM VICARY

The job was too good. There had to be a problem – and there was.

John Duncan was an honest man, but he needed money. He had children to look after. He was ready to do anything, and his bosses knew it.

They gave him the job because he couldn't say no; he couldn't afford to be honest. And the job was like a poison inside him. It changed him and blinded him, so that he couldn't see the real poison – until it was too late.